GOOD MANAGEMENT IS NOT FIREFIGHTING

JOEL QUASS

INFI∞ITY
PUBLISHING

Copyright © 2011 by Joel Quass

Library of Congress Control Number: 2010940085

www.goodmanagementisnot.com

Editing by Jeanne Ainslie, managing editor of West Coast Editing
www.westcoastediting.com

ISBN 0-7414-6326-1

Printed in the United States of America

Published January 2011

INFINITY PUBLISHING
1094 New DeHaven Street, Suite 100
West Conshohocken, PA 19428-2713
Toll-free (877) BUY BOOK
Local Phone (610) 941-9999
Fax (610) 941-9959
Info@buybooksontheweb.com
www.buybooksontheweb.com

Dave,

Thanks for making the time to speak with me. Best wishes for continued success!

Contents

Acknowledgments

I have had so many mentors and have learned so much from them that it is hard to begin to list them all.

Obviously, without a fire truck, the whole firefighting idea would be harder to imagine, so I want to first thank Ex-Chief Kevin McLaughin and the Point Pleasant Borough Fire Company No. 2, Ocean County Station 41, Point Pleasant, New Jersey for letting their trucks come "out and play." They are an all volunteer fire department that responds to approximately 300 to 350 calls a year, and they could use your support (Ocean County Station 41, 1206 Beaver Dam Road, Point Pleasant, NJ 08742).

Thanks also to Andy Castellani and the Forked River Fire Department for the fire hose piece. They are also a volunteer company that could use your support (www. forkedriverfire.com).

I am grateful to Best Products Company Inc. managers for teaching particularly Chuck Baber, Gary French for taking a chance and promoting me before I knew what I was doing, Bud Osbourne, Terry Thorne, Barry Pierce and Ken Collins for demonstrating good management techniques day in and day out.

At Costco, I am indebted to my colleagues Ken Acardi, Tom Albano, Don Amato, Reid Cardon, Michelle Cavette, Al Collins Sr., Rob Coope, John Cousanelli, Zack Davisson, Steve Deany, Bruce Deizendorf, Dean Desabrais, John Dougherty, Rick Duffy, Deborah Eckstein, Omar El Fashny, Mike Freeman, Steven Greever, David Jackson, Lorry Janus, Gary Kasdan, the Keating Brothers (Chuck, Jim and Don), Jeff Kenney, Skip Leonhard, Judith Logan, Eric Lund, Jim Mack, Randy Mazzotti, Steve Meyer, Debbie Quilty, Roy Rodenburg, Kevin Rusnak, Adam Self, Ken Shirley, Mike Shuff, Jim Stafford, John Van Burger, Billy Wallace, Leonard Wohlgemuth, Denny Woods and all the hundreds of salaried managers and hourly employees that I've had the privilege of learning from over the years.

Through Costco, my family and I have had many opportunities opened to us thanks to the support of Jim Sinegal, Joe Portera, Jeff Long, Roger Campbell, Yoram Rubanenko, Rob Leuck, Paul Pulver and Rich Wilcox.

A special thanks to Russ Miller, Mike "Bart" Bartoldus and Brian Minion for mentoring and helping me grow and to Justin Callahan for hiring me.

I am grateful to SCORE®, who provide small business mentoring and training, for showing my brother Brian and me basic business start-up ideas as we began our Quassword Card Business.

Many thanks to Kiera McKee and my daughter Cynthia for the fire truck photos.

I thank my children, Parker, Jonathan and Cynthia, my wife Nancy, and other family members for putting up with my repeatedly asking them "What do you think about this?" or "How does this sound?"

Finally, my thanks to *www.tracyharmanphotography.com* for the photo shoot that is now a line of motivational posters.

CHAPTER 1

Applying Common Sense

As Scott closed the hood of the car and asked for the cash, I knew something wasn't right. He had charged the customer for two quarts of oil, yet the rack was still full. As the woman drove away from the pump, I asked my employee what had happened.

Scott said, "Well, she thought she needed oil and so I checked and she didn't, but she really seemed like she wanted to buy oil, so I told her I put two quarts in and pocketed the money."

Wow, I thought to myself, That's crazy. I would never have thought to do something like that.

"That's stealing," I said to Scott.

"It's more a community service thing," he said, "since she really wanted to buy oil. If I didn't put oil in her car, someone else would."

This oil incident was my first test as a manager. I had worked through high school pumping gas nights and weekends, and now I was the manager of a gas station down the road. All I wanted to do was put away some money for a trip cruising the Inter-coastal Waterway on my sailboat the following spring. I had taken the job as station manager because it paid a little more. I thought, How hard can it be? Isn't being the manager really just a glorified employee who writes the schedule? I had no idea how much there was to learn.

Jump forward 35 years. My wife's Tai Chi instructor was teaching the class a new form. They were learning to Part Wild Horse's Mane on both Sides. My wife watched the demonstration of the new form and then said, "This looks just like Cloud Hands."

The instructor said, "Basically it is the same, there are only so many ways the body can move."

Across town at a political rally, a candidate gave a speech. After the speech a woman in the audience said, "She spoke for a lot of us. She just reinforced what we already knew."

And that's what I will be doing in the following chapters, reminding you of what you already know. I'm also going to tell you that there aren't any new ideas in management theory. There are just new ways of looking at the same concepts. This is really exciting because this means you already possess the basic information to be a successful manager.

But you're saying, "How can I know about business and management when I haven't been to business school, and I don't have an MBA."

But you have been through all the situations that you will face. Maybe it was in a classroom dealing with your 6th grade math teacher. Or at a used car lot dealing with a pushy and aggressive salesman. You have figured out a way to keep from overdrawing your checkbook, and you understand budgeting because you pay your personal bills on time. You have dealt with telemarketer phone calls and in-laws, and relatives who wanted your opinion or you to do things for them. Maybe they wanted to borrow money, or perhaps you wanted to borrow money from them. You have developed ways of handling these encounters. You are where you are in your life because you have some sort of strategy. You just might not be thinking of it that way.

All of us filter what we see and hear through our own personal paradigm or model of how the world works. When things fit your model, then you get it. When they don't, you may find yourself confused, angry, afraid, stuck, or lost. You seek additional information to make what you are working on fit your model. When you finally find the right pieces, then you get that "aha moment" where you once again get it. Then all is right with the world, and you can move on.

People say, "Well you know, management isn't rocket science." And I say, "Maybe it really is rocket science." I know what rocket science is because my father was a research engineer at Picatinny Arsenal in New Jersey where he specialized in solid rocket propellant. Then he joined NASA when they first started and spent 30 years developing solid rocket fuels for the Scout Rocket, a launch vehicle used to put satellites in orbit around the earth. He also oversaw the development of the propellant that shot the parachute out of the first Mars Lander. So I know a bit about rocket science from listening to my father talk about his work. I even accompanied him to Wallops Island, Virginia to see one of the Scout rocket launches. Getting a business off the ground and keeping it flying can be similar to putting a satellite in orbit.

Most of what my Dad did was research and planning. He had to know in advance what was most likely to happen. He had to know the forces acting on the rocket, starting with gravity. When you manage a business, you are anticipating and planning. You are making decisions all the time based on the information you have collected. When Neil Armstrong was about to land on the moon, he made a decision to override the computer guidance system and land the lunar module manually. He had had years of practice in the simulator, and when he saw the size of the boulders in the area that the computer was targeting for landing, he knew he had to act. As a manager, when you see an employee acting in a manner that jeopardizes your business, you act. Why? Because you already have years of real life experience to alert you to anything that could be bad for your business.

That same understanding can also give you the confidence to encourage an employee to act independently. You know from experience that they will make the same decision you would because you have taught them what is important to the company.

So how do we apply this to good management? Since you have this model (filter) from experience, you test everything to see how it fits with what you know to be true. Most of the time you are doing this unconsciously; your mind is searching back to situations similar to what you now face. You might not think that you can do this when you have a client in front of your face who is agitated because your company is behind in shipping the one component needed to complete their new line of silk dresses. But you have years of practice dealing with children, parents, neighbors, co-workers, your boss, and friends when they are upset. You know how to listen; let them get it all out until they have nothing else to say. And that's usually the key; they want to be heard. Then it is your turn to be empathetic, to restate what they have said, and then to work on a solution that is beneficial to both parties. You may not recognize that you have it, but it's there! And you already know that. So I want to talk about good management and help remind you of what it takes to be successful.

When one thinks of management in the broad sense, you may think MBAs, or you probably have heard of *The Practice of Management* by Peter Drucker, or *The One*

Minute Manager by Ken Blanchard. Speaking of one minute managing, I once held a "One Minute Meeting" inside an empty 54 ft. trailer attached to a loading dock. I was the opening senior manager at a large box retailer, and when I arrived at 6 a.m. I found that the first two hours had been less than productive. I turned on my walkie-talkie in the parking lot and overheard two managers going at it over the radio concerning how much freight was coming to the floor that morning and who was responsible for getting the building open on time. As I came in the back door, I called every manager in the building to the dock, marched them into the empty trailer and pulled the roll-up door down behind me. Turning around, their faces showed intense concentration, and a touch of terror. I asked a couple of quick, specific questions about the morning and then gave some clear direction. I then turned, rolled the door up and sent them back out to the floor. The rest of the morning ran smoothly, and they actually accomplished more than their original plans. In addition, all the freight was put away earlier than usual. I can't really take credit for their success; my managers just needed to be refocused. They were very good at what they did, but they had allowed employee call outs and a few little hiccups to escalate into a free-for-all. Pulling them all aside in an unexpected way grabbed their attention, and they were then able to concentrate on the immediate job.

But millions of years before Peter Drucker and Ken Blanchard, the first managers were the early cavemen who organized their tribes into hunters and gathers. The stakes were much different in those days. I can imagine our caveman receiving a corrective from his boss, the tribal elder. "Ugh, I brought you into my office today to discuss your recent performance in the wooly mammoth hunt coordinated with the Smoke River Clan over the mountain. As you know, your failure to follow policy 6-A on page 47 of the employee agreement resulted in the death of two of our hunting party, including the son of one of our senior managers in the spear-making division. Policy 6-A states you will not place hunters between the prey and the side of a cliff. Since you decided to do that anyway, I am going to have to give you a verbal corrective consultation. If this happens again, I will be forced to give you a written consultation. But I'm sure that won't be necessary, since you are generally a good supervisor and a team player. But if it does happen again, then per company policy, I will be forced to suspend you for three days without pay. And Ugh, if you can't get this under control, and our fellow hunters keep getting killed, I will be forced to fire you. I'm sure that you don't want that to happen, so can I get your word that you will follow company policies going forward? OK, just put your mark here and return to your post as leader of the saber tooth tiger scouting party."

Failure to follow the manager's directions in those days didn't result first in a verbal, then a written corrective outlining areas of concern, followed by an unpaid suspension, and finally termination. In prehistoric society, failure to follow management's directives usually resulted in banishment from the tribe or death. There were obvious advantages to following directions and not challenging authority.

Management principles developed very slowly until the 6th century BC when the Chinese General, Sun Tzu, wrote *The Art of War*. While it was written as a military strategy book, the lessons have been applied to many things over the centuries, including management practice and theory. For managerial purposes, the application is being aware of and acting on strengths and weaknesses of both a manager's organization and a foe's.[1]

In 1904, Ida Tarbell in her book, *History of the Standard Oil Company,* unintentionally illustrates the *Art of War* as applied to the creation of the oil business. "With Mr. Rockefeller's genius for detail, there went a sense of the big and vital factors in the oil business, and a daring in laying hold of them which was very like military genius. He saw strategic points like a Napoleon, and he swooped on them with the suddenness of a Napoleon. . . . The man saw what was necessary to his purpose, and he never hesitated before it. His courage was steady-and his faith in his ideas unwavering. He simply knew that was the thing to do, and he went ahead with the serenity of the man who knows."[2]

When, as a manager, you have an "ah-ha moment", you are tapping into that creative energy that Sun Tzu was talking about. It is that energy and drive that makes you successful and drives your business. Regardless of your position in your company, if you think of the business as yours, you will always make the right decision.

In 1513 Niccolò Machiavelli wrote *The Prince* where he recommended to the leaders of Florence, Italy that they use fear, not hatred, to maintain control. I still see elements of this in managers today. First you win over the masses (your employees) by some act, and then you show them the consequences of disobedience. Fearing those consequences, they act in their best interest, complying with the demands and orders of the king, or company president, division chief or department manager (whatever your title is). When they comply, they protect themselves, which is in their best interest and that produces the result you are after. This only works as long as the fear is real and the consequences are sure and immediate. Once you begin to play favorites, cracks in the armor appear and a new leader emerges and offers to win over the masses (your employees), and the cycle begins anew, only this time it is without you.

In the late 1800's, economists Alfred Marshall and Léon Walras introduced a new complexity to management theory. Mary Parker Follett (1868–1933) defined management as "the art of getting things done through people."[3] In 1881, Joseph Wharton, a Philadelphia industrialist and philanthropist, founded the world's first collegiate business school. In 1911, J. Duncan wrote the first college management textbook, *The Principles of Industrial Management.* The Harvard Business School invented the Master of Business Administration degree (MBA) in 1921. The various branches of management and their interrelationships were studied using the principles of psychology and sociology. H. Dodge, Ronald Fisher, and Thorton C. Fry introduced statistical techniques to management studies. In the 1940s, Patrick Blackett combined statistics theory with microeconomic theory to create operations research (management science). Recent developments include the Theory of Constraints, management by objectives, reengineering, Six Sigma, agile software development, and group management theories such as Cog's ladder.

Today, business management consists of six branches, namely, human resources management, operations management, strategic management, marketing management, financial management, and information technology management (IT). Management theory also exists for, nonprofits and government branches, such as public administration, public management, and educational management. Management functions are usually described as planning, organizing, staffing, leading/directing, controlling/monitoring, and motivating.

Even with all this attention given to management theory since Peter Drucker's first book, you still hear management described as "what managers do." If that is the definition, then it's no wonder newly promoted managers don't know what their job is. And don't forget Lee Iacocca's famous quote "Management is nothing more than motivating other people."[4] We will look at this more closely in the section on leadership, but for now, remember this. Management has been around since cavemen first organized to increase their productivity, while formal management theory is just over 100 years old. To manage means to run, direct, administer, supervise, handle, deal with, or control. This is what most management job descriptions outline, a series of tasks to perform for the business to be successful. Your job as a manager is to get your people to perform these tasks in such a way that they increase sales or decrease expenses. In the following chapters, we will examine ideas that will help you to be successful when faced with seemingly daunting assignments. We will examine ways you can expand your model of how things work by applying what you already know to be true to these new situations.

CHAPTER 2

Good Management
Is Not
Firefighting

What could be more thrilling than a fast-paced business environment where problems are being hurled at you one after another, and you are standing in the middle of this chaos barking orders, controlling every activity so that it ends up exactly as you foresaw it? You are the master of all you see, the ultimate authority in your field, the king (or queen) of the realm. None of your employees dare make a move without consulting you. You stand taller and see further into the future than any of the managers or hourly employees who report to you. When the flames of a problem rear their ugly head, you are there with the fire extinguisher, ready to douse the flames and restore order. And when there are no flames, you might even unknowingly toss a match here or there. For what good is ultimate power if you don't get to use it. After all, you are THE MANAGER. You worked hard to get where you are. And the last thing you want is trouble. Yet, by focusing on not having trouble, that's exactly what you get. But who better to deal with trouble than you? So the circle of life is complete; you get trouble and you put it out. You feel good that you have solved a problem, so you go looking for another fire. Soon you are fiddling while Rome is burning. And you can't understand why your business is not more successful.

In order to see what is going on behind the scenes, you must learn to deal with all types of employees and managers. Getting to the core of the problem sometimes means understanding where they are coming from. This reminds me of Lin-Chi's saying, "When you meet a master swordsman, show him your sword. When you meet a man who is not a poet, do not show him your poem."[5] It's one thing when your employees are this way, but it can be harder to deal with your boss when she is a master swordswoman.

Ginger never took no for an answer. It was her way or the highway. There was a drive in her, and it was all business. I watched many managers over the years deal with Ginger. The good thing about Ginger was that you always knew where you stood. There was never a question about what she expected, or whose responsibility it was to get something done. If you kept your sword out, you were respected. But bring out that poem and you could be eaten alive. Ginger had a soft side, but she never showed it unless there were no witnesses. She could tell you in private that you made the right decision in dealing with a customer or an employee situation, but she would never acknowledge it in front of other managers. Dealing with this type of personality is simple; keep it all business unless they bring up something else. Then comment sparingly and get back to business. I once overheard her, in private in her office, complimenting Fred, a manager, for a decision he had made concerning one of the company's clients. Company policy stated not to give credit to a branch for defective merchandise unless it was ordered through that branch. A manager was required to direct the client to the office where the merchandise was ordered.

However, this particular client also placed large orders with Fred, who understood that his client saw only one company, not individual profit centers that would be negatively impacted by the credit. You see, in Ginger's eyes, it was all about her area being profitable. If someone else was supposed to take the margin hit, then they should. At least that's what she said in front of the staff and the manager who took care of his client. But later, in private, Ginger told Fred she thought he had made the right decision. So keep your sword out, but keep your eyes on what's right for the customer, and you will survive encounters with your own Ginger.

You may have worked for a manager like this, or you may have an employee who is hard to reach. If you do not figure out how to get through to this employee, you end up firefighting and never end up getting the most out of your employee. Or worse, you are always frustrated with the employee and eventually drive them from the organization, not on purpose, but by failing to reach them. You end up thinking that they don't get it, but they do. They see that they are not receiving support or training in a way that they understand. So they become just as frustrated as you are and become a thorn in your side, or they leave. Remember the 80/20 Rule?

The 80/20 Rule states that as a manager, you will spend 80% of your time dealing with 20% of the employees. That sounds like a great ratio until you realize that the 20% are often not your stellar employees. They are the needy employees—they need questions answered, their hands held, time off, specific schedules, a different responsibility, a new title, a day off to visit Mom. These employees are sometimes lovingly referred to as high maintenance. Yet some of the 20% are actually good performers when things are right. As for the rest of the 20%, they seem to know what buttons to push and just how far to go before they cross the line. They can consume the manager's energy, draining him or her until the manager has little left to give to the other 80% of the employees who are doing a good or excellent job. Because the 20% are in-your-face obvious, it is easy to lose track of and not recognize all the good things going on with the other employees. Any system that encourages positive recognition will help to keep the 80% engaged.

Managers having to deal with a 20% employee may try to dodge that employee. "Oh no, here comes John. I'll run to the bathroom, and maybe he won't see me." Of course, who ends up in the stall next to that manager? John. And now the manager is cornered. Usually by giving them a chance to vent and then redirecting their concerns to a more constructive approach, this type of employee will feel included and willing to give their best. As I said, sometimes these are great employees, but you have to be able to manage them. This includes being able to anticipate their concerns and address them in advance. And by that I don't mean running and hiding in the bathroom.

Howard Coonley from Sprint/Nextel was quoted as saying, "The executive of the future will be rated by his ability to anticipate his problems rather than to meet them as they come."[6] Successful managers make the time to plan for the future instead of waiting for it to arrive. I know a manager who describes managers who fail to plan "as rolling the dice, crossing their fingers, and hoping for the best." If you are shooting craps in Atlantic City, maybe that's all you can do. But if your company's reputation is on the line, and your department is responsible for the main segment of a presentation to a client, the last thing you can afford to do is just roll the dice. Yet I see managers do this all the time. And they don't even realize they are doing it. It begins when they are assigned the project. They spend a few minutes reviewing their notes from the last project, which only takes a few minutes because they really don't have any notes. They have some things they remember from a similar project about 11 months ago, but they didn't make any notes, or the notes are not where they can find them. So even before they have begun the new project, they have set themselves up to have the same result as last time. Now if the last time they received the contract and they were the hero, then life is good. But usually there was at least one area that could have been improved. A part of the presentation that did not go as smoothly or something that was remembered after the fact that would have closed the deal quicker. Without that information, this manager is standing in front of her latest project, crossing her fingers, rolling the dice and hoping for the best.

Author Gustav Metzman said, "Most business men generally are so busy coping with immediate and piecemeal matters that there is a lamentable tendency to let the long run or future take care of itself. We are often so busy putting out fires, so to speak, that we find it difficult to do the planning that would prevent those fires from occurring in the first place."[7]

After spending a day firefighting, you go home ex-hausted. But you think back and say "I sure did a lot today! I was all over the place taking care of business. I saved a lot of people." Yet in reality, the day would have been much smoother and more productive if there had been a focus on why things were happening. Why did you spend 45 minutes with George? Were you giving him the tools to do his job, or were you doing his job for him? When Jennifer alerted you to a problem in finance, did you solve the problem? Or did you get the section chief involved, work through the issue with him, and show him how to avoid a similar problem in the future?

Probably not. People want to be needed, and the surest way to be needed is to be a firefighter. "Hey, we've got a small blaze over here! Call, Jim. He knows how to put that out." Jim may also know in the back of his mind how to keep the fire from popping up again, but if he does that, what will he do to pass his time at work? After all, he's very good at putting out fires.

Until you start seeing the results of your teaching, you will continue to fight fires. Once you can see how teaching someone to avoid having the fire start in the first place is in your best interest, you will actually set a new goal of *not having fires in the first place*. This will set you apart from others in the organization, result in promotion, advancement, raises, and increased impact on how your company moves forward. Hey, you might be perceived as a hero just for taking the time to teach your employees how to do their jobs and by teaching them how to avoid starting fires. Yet, even when you do this, there is always someone out there who has different ideas.

In any company that has more than two employees, there is the potential to have an arsonist in the mix. You've seen them, I'm sure. You know right away when Christine comes to you with that look on her face that she has already lit the match and set a pile of gas soaked rags on fire. She's only coming to you because you don't know that they are on fire, and so you are not jumping up and down yet yelling, "Someone get a bucket of water and put out that fire!" The arsonist now gets to watch the action unfold; everyone running around because of something he or she caused. But every good arsonist does such a great job of disguising their actions that it seems to the untrained eye as if someone else set the blaze. They paint themselves as the innocent bystander who just happened by as the first flames were appearing. You know in your heart that they set the blaze, but proving it is another matter. Generally you are so busy putting out the fire and dealing with the collateral damage that you leave no time to investigate the situation and find out what really happened. Being a firefighter shows we are on top of things; we are handling the situation. Taking on the role of the crime scene (CSI) investigator takes more time and energy—it means actually sitting down and talking to employees, taking written statements, and seeing if there were any witnesses. Then you review all the material and form a conclusion, meet with your employees to let them know what you have found and then issue counseling notices or possibly start the termination process, which involves additional paperwork. Who wants to do all that work? Isn't it easier to just turn on the hose, spray everybody down and then head back to the fire station?

Most managers and supervisors want to do the right thing, but they don't have the courage or self-confidence. They fear confrontation; they shy away from facing the real issue because they have to make decisions and be held accountable in the same way that they will hold the arsonist accountable. By not going after the source of the blaze, they avoid having to deal with the real problem. It's much more comfortable. It's easy to think, I don't get paid enough to deal with this, or I think Oscar started this fire, but Gwen is saying she saw Brittany nearby and that Joseph was really there before either of them. You know Brittany is the type of employee who always has an answer for everything, and if you bring her into the office to discuss this, you might as well cancel all you appointments for the rest of the day. And Gwen will think you are picking on her, and Joseph does such a good job in so many areas that you don't want to confront him for fear he will pull back from the great job he is doing. So there you are—you have an arsonist in your midst. You have a strong feeling you really know what is going on, but you choose not to address it. You probably do not even realize that you are not addressing the real problem because after all didn't you just put out the fire? You saved the organization today by being there when they needed you. And by covering the problem in fire retardant foam, you have successfully smothered the problem, haven't you? Unfortunately, fires can smolder after the flames are gone. Even covered in ash, the coals of last night's campfire can start a new blaze just by blowing off the ash and applying a little dry kindling. So it's tomorrow or next week or sometime in the future when something else very important is taking place that the flames from this old fire break out, and the process starts all over again. But this time you are right in the middle of a huge deadline and you don't get to turn the water on the flames until it's a 3-alarm blaze. Now your boss is asking what's going on, and the fire commissioner, your boss's boss, is on the phone wanting to know how this started, and why wasn't he aware of it? And now you are the one in the office being talked to about how this fire started and why it wasn't addressed.

So I suggest you toss the fire helmet in the closet and dig into the real problem. But don't worry; even in the best run organizations, there are always times when you get to wear the fire helmet. It's just that you won't get very far in your company if that's all you do. Search for the source of the problem, not the symptoms.

CHAPTER 3

Good Management
Is Not
Being the Hero

William Fromm, author of *Ten Commandments of Business and How to Break Them* recommended, "If you want your people (*employees*)[8] to deliver outstanding customer service, you need to treat them as if they were more important than the customers. The problem is no one sits down with us to explain this new philosophy when we get promoted into management."

I always try to follow Fromm's advice. But I see far too many managers who don't use their employees as a valuable asset, but rather as a means to an end. This is reminiscent of the turn of the century factories where workers had no rights, and the manager had total say about nearly everything connected with a person's employment.

Labor unions began to evolve in the United States in the 1700s and 1800s due to the need for safety and security for workers. Workers formed labor unions in response to intolerable working conditions, low wages, and long hours.[9] A labor union is defined as "a group of workers who have banded together to achieve common goals in the key areas of wages, hours, and working conditions."[10]

During the twentieth century, however, laws have been passed that guarantee employees many of the rights that once had to be negotiated in labor management contracts. An increase in employee-management teamwork and communication has also reduced the need for workers to be represented by labor unions. Thus, labor unions no longer play the vital role they once did in American labor-management relations.[9]

I bring this up because the same conditions that created the need for labor unions have not completely vanished from the American workforce. It is more subtle and hard to see, but elements are still there. Some individual managers still run their operations modeled after the same workplace rules that led to the creation of labor unions. In most cases, the workers' safety and personal security are not at risk, but with all the tools available to managers today, it is disappointing to see managers reverting to the "I am the manager, and you do as I say" philosophy. This does nothing to empower employees or create a sense of ownership about the project and build loyalty to the company and manager. However, I believe that we shall continue to see successful workplaces grow because of the employees and their managers who create a work environment that fosters innovation and collaboration.

Sam came to me the other day. He had asked his immediate manager for a day off to see his ailing grandmother. His boss had reminded him that there was a blackout period in effect for time-off requests since this was our busiest season. The manager said, "There is nothing I can do, but if you like, you can talk to my boss." So now the employee is in front of me asking for the day off. Hmm, if I am going to solve problems one-on-one with his employees, *then why do I need a department manager?* I could save the payroll and do it myself. Yet many managers play the "it is out of my hands" card or the "company policy" card and do not think about the consequences of not solving their own departmental problem. One good thing the department manager did was mention the open-door policy. Otherwise, he gave up control of his department, and the next time that employee needs anything, he will probably bypass the department manager and come directly to me. So what did I do with Sam? I told him I would review the situation with his boss and have his boss get back to him. Then I called his boss to my office and explained ownership. I walked him through how he could say to Sam, "I can understand why it is important to you that you see your ailing grandmother. Let me see what I can do to accommodate your request, even though we are in a blackout period. I will get back to you this afternoon with an answer." Then the department manager, Sam's boss, could have come to see me and discussed the issue. Together we could have figured out how to help this employee. Then the department manager would have gone back to the employee and given the employee *his* decision. The next time this employee needs something, he will see his department manager, his boss, as a problem solver and a person he can go to. As a side benefit for the department manager in the future, this employee is also more likely to apply a little extra effort to help his manager when extra help is needed because of how he was treated. Now he sees his boss as the hero. This is better for me because now his manager will be able to handle future employee requests without my direct involvement, and I can concentrate on bigger picture issues, such as driving sales and reducing expenses.

Employee empowerment has received a lot of press, but not all organizations have embraced the concept. One company that did was General Electric (GE). In 1981, when Jack Welch was appointed CEO of GE, its market cap was about $12 billion. When he stepped down as CEO in 2000, GE's market cap had grown to $500 billion. Jack followed his Seven Point Program for Management by Leadership. Point 5 was Empower Individuals.[11] With such success, one would think that all companies would build the same corporate infrastructure. But I have talked with many mid-level managers who are afraid to speak up in meetings, afraid

30

to make a decision. Sadly, most of the time these managers would make the correct decision, but they haven't been encouraged to speak up, or supported when they do. Their manager may be waiting for them to say something, but she hasn't empowered them or established a structure that allows for input or suggestions. So she makes the decision and moves ahead. Her employees are not very enthusiastic about the project because they have ideas that they haven't expressed. Sometimes they might have ideas that would actually move the project forward faster, saving money or increasing sales. By not valuing her employees, this manager has lost valuable input.

Steven A. Cohen, a self-made billionaire, trades stocks on his 180-person trading floor in Stamford, Connecticut. He and 100 portfolio managers buy and sell 100 million shares a day. This is about one percent of all shares traded on US exchanges. According to a February 26, 2010 online article in *Bloomberg Markets Magazine*, if a portfolio manager or analyst can't answer a question about a stock, Cohen is likely to lash out. "Do you even know how to do this f---ing job?"[12] is a standard barb, current and former employees say. This extreme management style is primarily the reason for the firm's incredible success over the years and the source of Mr. Cohen's fortune. In fact, he keeps the trading floor temperature below 70 to keep his brokers from dozing. The cost of his success with this unique management style is that he has huge turnover; most of his brokers last less than four years. This strategy was what made Mr. Cohen a billionaire, but he churns through his employees, not as individuals, but as a line item expense that is just a part of doing business.

Managers who emulate this style in organizations can be very effective in achieving a specific result by a specific deadline, but the cost is usually low morale and high turnover. Upper management can sometimes see only the results and not the cost of such an aggressive style, and these managers are promoted. But there is a difference between holding employees accountable and driving them to the edge. A balanced approach of teaching and feedback often results in a more productive group of employees over time. This management style also brings recognition and promotion. The costs are different because you are investing more time in teaching and follow-up. As an *extreme* manager, however, most of your time is spent on the follow-up, with the expectation that the employees already know what you expect and should be slaving at this very moment to produce what you want. Employees who do not understand exactly what you want will many times guess because they are afraid to ask, in case you snap at them and ask why they don't already know. As a result, they spiral downward and produce less and less, requiring you to spend more and more time with them until they quit, transfer, or pass away unexpectedly.

Atul Gawande, in his book, *The Checklist Manifesto: How to Get Things Right*, explains how some industries have business models that require employee feedback—input from all parties is built into the process. He describes the building plans for a 15-storey building that was to be built on soft earth. The plan was to build the interior columns before the exterior walls were attached. As the construction project moved ahead, they noticed after a heavy rain that water was collecting in the center of the building. The floor was not level. What did they do? They called all the subcontractors together and discussed the situation. They actively sought input to resolve the issue. They concluded that the floor would become level after they hung the exterior walls—the weight was temporarily unevenly distributed across the structure. And in the end, after the construction was complete, the building floors were level. When this problem arose, it wasn't the site manager himself who made the decision. The organizational structure of his business required that anyone who had input into the building plans be involved. Most corporate structures do not have a formal process involving all relevant employees or departments when reviewing problems. But that doesn't mean you can't have a plan in place yourself to deal with unplanned problems. Don't be like Linus in George Schultz's "Peanuts." Linus is talking to Charlie Brown and says, "I don't like to face problems head on. I think the best way to solve problems is to avoid them. This is a distinct philosophy of mine. . . . No problem is so big or so complicated that it can't be run away from."

Earlier, I talked about the cavemen and how they organized themselves. I am reminded of the GEICO Cavemen commercial "so easy, a caveman can do it." Well I'm not sure how easy it was for cavemen to organize and for effective managers to emerge, but I'm sure they quickly learned the benefits of organizational structure. Newly promoted managers may feel that their job is easy—they walk around and tell other people what to do. Why? They're the boss. Promoted to a position with programs currently in place, the new manager just needs to keep these running to be successful, at least in the short-term. But when the manager has that first interaction with an employee who requires something that is not clearly addressed in the company policies and procedures, the new manager has to actually make a decision that has consequences. Now they are putting themselves on the line. They have the chance to be the hero, or to give the credit to one of their employees. They can empower and begin building goodwill between themselves and their staff, or they can grab the glory and alienate the very people who will ultimately be responsible for their success or failure as a manager.

But more importantly, when you empower your employees to be the hero and contribute to the company's success, they feel alive and important. This attitude should be encouraged, not stifled. Your goal is to make your employees feel confident so that they can face problems and make decisions. Dale Carnegie wrote "every great organization is the lengthened shadow of one man."[13] If your employees are in tune with what you want and feel empowered to do what you want without reprisal, then they will act in a given situation the same way you would. They become the "shadow of a leader," and that leader is you. Robert Greenleaf, a noted leadership and management theorist, said "Good leaders must first become good servants."[14] This is in a similar spirit to the quote by William Fromm at the beginning of this chapter. In fact, it bears repeating, "If you want your people to deliver outstanding customer service, then you need to treat them as if they were more important than the customers."[15] It is easy to forget this if you want to be the decision maker. After all, that's what being the manager is all about, right? But taking away your employees' chances to participate and make decisions also takes away their ownership of the situation and eventually their willingness to go the extra mile when business demands increase. If you encourage your employees to make decisions and have given them the proper guidelines, then you have given them power. This scares some managers. If they give away their power, what do they have left? But this is very narrow-minded, because the moment you give power to your employees, you get it back in goodwill and your employees' ownership in the decision and its consequences. This goodwill is more valuable than wearing the manager title in completing tasks through others and effectively managing.

As managers we have a choice to make each time we deal with our employees. We can build trust, respect, and develop our company's future leaders, or we can see the situation as a chance to protect our own *assets* and steal the glory from the employee. This may work in the short-term, but in the long-term, your employees' success, (because you developed them) will be the stepping-stone to your promotion. Remember, most of your job as a manager is teaching. You are the one responsible for how your employees handle any given situation. When you teach them the correct way, the way you would do it, you are setting standards. When you actually hold your employees accountable to this standard, you give them feedback. If they do not perform correctly, you coach, counsel, and document until they do it correctly. Then you praise them. Now you have employees who will do what you would do; you have taught them how to be successful, and at the same time you have demonstrated to the company your ability to get things done through other people. In other words, you are an effective manager.

CHAPTER 4

Good Management
Is Not
Single-Handed

As I turned around, I saw my boss enter the office with an 8-lb sledge hammer in his hands. "Out of the way," he yelled. As I cleared the doorway, I watched him march over to the locked two-drawer filing cabinet that housed all the employee files. "Wham" went the sledge hammer as it hit the corner of the filing cabinet. "Open you so and so," I heard him mutter under his breath, and then "Wham" a second time. This time the lock popped, and the filing cabinet yielded the file my boss needed.

My management career began almost 35 years ago. Believe me, I had no idea what I was getting myself into. My ideas of my responsibilities have most certainly changed along the way. And as they changed, I began to notice how others in the profession responded to situations. Thinking, I can always learn something from someone who knows more than I do—as Ralph Waldo Emerson said, "In every man there is something wherein I may learn of him, and in that I am his pupil."[16] As a result, I began to study other managers and watch for successful behaviors that I could imitate. One manager that I worked for stands out in particular. Yes, the one I learned the most from did wield a sledge hammer in the office. It turned out that the payroll clerk had accidentally taken the keys home, and he needed information that was in that cabinet only. I have said many times that I have learned things from him I will *always* do, and I have also learned things from him that I will *never* do. But I have seen employees, supervisors, and managers come to him for help and guidance because he really knows how to teach. He taught me how to get things done through other people. He is the kind of guy that makes sure you have the tools to do your job while holding you accountable for using them to complete the job.

While I have never hit a locked filing cabinet with an 8-lb sledge hammer, I have used many tools that this manager taught me. He was not afraid to delegate, and he also showed me the importance of systematic follow-up to our business success. He understood that without keeping in touch with the employees that he delegated work to, he was at their mercy and would have to accept whatever they produced. It is not surprising that this man is now a vice-president in the organization. Jack Welsh, former CEO of General Electric said, "Follow up on everything. Follow-up is one key measure of success for a business. Your follow-up business strategy will pave the way for your success."[11]

Delegation and follow-up are two basic elements of successful management. Many managers are great at delegating, but never seem to get around to the follow-up. Then they are surprised when the project is not completed by the deadline, or the event doesn't come off as planned. They blame the employee for lack of success instead of seeing that their lack of follow-up and direction was the problem. It's much easier to blame others than to accept responsibility for your actions. In reality, employee short-falls should be a clear sign to management that they (the managers) have not clearly defined the job expectations and that the employee really needs more information delivered in a way that they can understand.

Another benefit of delegating is the vast improvement in productivity that specialization can achieve. In 1776, Adam Smith wrote *An Inquiry into the Nature and Causes of the Wealth of Nations*. There he demonstrated how productive a team of workers could be if tasks were delegated to a specific individual. Smith found that there were 18 individual steps in making a hat pin. A skilled worker in a pin factory could produce 200 pins per day. At that rate, 10 workers could produce 2,000 pins in one day. However, if you broke the 18 tasks apart and assigned them to individual workers, with the 10 employees each responsible for only one or two steps in the pin-making process, they could produce 48,000 pins per day.

Such productivity gains were almost unimaginable. Did someone say Industrial Revolution? This way of thinking was revolutionary at the time. Having the courage to think about any current process in a new way is revolutionary. Yet even as these gains were being made in factories all over the civilized world, there were managers who were fighting against the same ideas.

Some managers will say it is easier to do it themselves than to take the time to explain the task to an employee. These are the same managers who complain that they never have enough time to get everything done or that their employees don't know what they are doing. Teaching is such an important part of the delegation process. Anyone can tell an employee, build me a time machine that will transport me backward or forward in time. You can even give that employee a deadline of say next Thursday. But how realistic is that goal? If the employee doesn't know what to do and you haven't taught them how to do this task, they may ask a fellow employee to help, which will make both employees less productive. The second employee may have built a time machine once, but he was working for a different company at the time, and his machine would only transport a person back in time. They had never worked out the bugs to bring people back to the present. So now you have something that may be ready by the deadline, but it is not usable for your purpose. And worse, you might not even recognize that it isn't what you want until you try it out. Now you have sent yourself back in time with no way to return.

Now, I know what you are thinking, we don't have time machines. But we do have employees who are told by their bosses to do things that they are not trained to do. And worse, the manager is surprised when the results are not what they expected. But did they ask the employee upfront if they know how to perform the task delegated to them? Did they follow-up with the employee at regular intervals to see what progress was being made? Did they create a work environment that would make the employee feel free to come and ask questions about the delegated task? Did the manager teach the employee what was needed to complete the task? If many of these answers are no, I'm sure you can guess what the end result will be.

Your company's mission statement, if carefully written, will give your employees direction when they must make decisions not clearly outlined in the company's policy and procedures manual. In a recent Harvard Business Review online article, Rosabeth Moss Kanter, Harvard Business School professor, talked about values and principles in crisis situations. "Clear standards and values can serve as a guidance system to steer decisions without sluggish bureaucracy. People know the right thing to do without being told and without waiting for permission. Proctor & Gamble (P&G) was the first organization to evacuate employees (and their families) from Lebanon after military action; the regional general manager was certain that the costs would be supported because of P&G's values."[17]

This type of empowerment can be great, and it doesn't have to be a life or death situation for your employees to make use of it. If your employees know that they have the power to resolve situations and will make the same decision you would, then you have given them the chance to be the hero, and you have saved yourself from being involved in every situation that is not exactly like the book. Employees who know what they can and can't do will perform with confidence and give your customers the best possible experience. When they understand your mission statement and are allowed and encouraged to apply it when interacting with customers, you are delegating the decision-making to your employees. They have the satisfaction of making decisions and resolving an issue for the customer. With your employees more engaged, you are free to look at the big picture that will grow your business or decrease your costs.

Another way to think of delegation and follow-up is the old adage: Inspect what you expect. It's amazing how employees can make something a priority when the boss thinks it's a priority. And even more amazing that this works when the moment before you didn't think it was a good idea or that it was even possible. Then the boss, or the boss's boss, comes for a visit and says, "This division is lagging behind the other three in my territory. You need to perform at a higher level. I will be back in four weeks, and I expect that you will be closing 17% more sales than you are currently. Your closing rate is 12 basis points below the division average, and in the past you have been the division leader. Get off your butts and make this happen." So you say, "OK."

Well you didn't mention to the boss's boss that Sally was out on maternity leave and that Jim was out for two more weeks due to an injury or that several of your key clients had recently been lured away by a competitor. Most people when challenged like this focus on figuring it out. They find a way to get out of the rut they are in and start to make things happen. When it's a priority to their boss, they stop making excuses and find a solution. Someone gets on the phone with the clients they lost and discovers that they really aren't happy. Suddenly, new orders come in. Then you decide on a little motivational contest and divide your division into teams—the Red, the White, and the Blue. Next you post sales information and contract closing rates for your division, by teams, as well as how you are doing against the larger territory. By the time four weeks have rolled around, the reasons why you weren't performing are long gone. The boss's boss comes back as promised, and you are there with your head held high. Not only are you closing 17% more sales, but the average contract is significantly higher than those from the other divisions. So what happened?

You stopped focusing on why you couldn't perform at a higher level, and you began to focus on *what you could do* to perform at a higher level. And then you did it. Your pride, your reputation was on the line. By the end of the four weeks, you had the bragging rights. You probably had called or sent emails to friends you know in the other divisions, gently suggesting that you were now kicking their butts. And not only did your division's performance improve, but by challenging your neighbors, you inadvertently increased sales in the other divisions. All of this was because someone in authority said something. Your boss's boss said, "This is important to me and I am going to come back and check on your progress in four weeks." While this results in a great feeling of accomplishment, the whole process is even more spectacular when you don't wait until the boss's boss tells you to do it.

You can challenge yourself, your department, and your staff with anything that needs a renewed focus. How much more satisfying is it to have the boss's boss call your boss and say, "What's going on in your division? In the past four weeks, you have increased your closing rate by 17%. What are you doing?" And then your boss can say, "Well (your name here) saw that we were lagging in sales, and so he started posting results and challenging the other managers in our division. He even broke the group up into teams and tracked how we were doing against the entire territory. We are currently challenging another division and expect to increase our closing rate even further over the next four weeks." What a great conversation to have. To have someone above you in the corporate hierarchy recognize that something good was going on in your area of responsibility. This will look good in your annual review, and people will remember that when they are looking for managers to promote. All because you inspected what you expected. You involved your employees—you helped them and taught them what they needed to know to close at a better rate. And you gave regular feedback about their performance, so that they could continue to improve.

The more successful you and your division became, the more fun the whole process became. Four weeks ago, you weren't all that excited about coming to work. You were complaining to yourself, "We're down 17% in closings against the rest of the territory, and we can't do better because my best people are out." Then one day you said, "Wait a minute. What if we tried something new? What if I put my focus on what I can do?" And the rest, as they say, is history. Remember, as Peter Drucker once said, "The productivity of work is not the responsibility of the worker but of the manager." By changing your attitude towards the work, you made your employees more productive.

CHAPTER 5

Good Management
Is Not
Non-Stop

Stress is the silent killer. Our bodies still respond to the "fight or flight" reflex ingrained in our ancestors millions of years ago. The need for that reflex reaction to situations is not always necessary in today's society, but our bodies have not yet evolved to the point where it can recognize the difference between facing a saber tooth tiger or a room full of potential investors. Managers who cannot set boundaries between their professional and personal lives risk early burn out. I'm sure every generation says, "In today's world we face different challenges from our parents' generation." But as instant messaging (IM) technology spreads, the line between work and play becomes even more blurred. We have moved past pagers, and now our cell phones are our constant companions, making us accessible to anyone—

friend, business associate, boss, bill collector, or phone solicitation for a service or contribution. We are on 24 hours a day. E-mail and apps (applications). are now common on most cell phones, and then there is Digg, My Space, Facebook, Delicious, LinkedIn and Twitter. An internal filter for your sanity is essential.

In his article "The Nature of Stress," Hans Selye, a famous endocrinologist and an expert in the field of stress management, defined stress as follows: "Stress is the nonspecific response of the body to any demand, whether it is caused by, or results in, pleasant or unpleasant conditions."[18] The American Institute of Stress (AIS) gives the dictionary definition of stress as "physical, mental, or emotional strain or tension," or "a condition or feeling experienced when a person perceives that demands exceed the personal and social resources the individual is able to mobilize (mainly attributed to the psychologist Richard S. Lazarus)."[19]

Sensory or stress overload leave us unable to act. While some people thrive in an extreme environment, many do not. But once again, all is not lost. Hans Selye reminds us that under the proper circumstances, the fight-or-flight response can be a good thing. The AIS states that "Stress can be helpful and good when it motivates people to accomplish more. . . . Increased stress results in increased productivity— up to a point."

The triggers that protected the early cave dwellers are still inside of us. How we respond to these stressors either helps us perform better or leaves us cowering in the corner, unable to face the situation and its consequences. While this can sound bad, the point is we have this response mechanism built into us, so the more we know about it, the better we can use stress to be productive, instead of incapacitating us.

One would think that Type A personalities are more at risk, but my experience is that their metabolism is better geared to most fast-paced business professions. It's the Type A wannabes who experience the most stress—trying to exchange their personality for one that they feel will give them an edge. Wannabes would do better if they understood and made the most of their own habits and traits—this would give them a greater chance of success with less physical and emotional damage to themselves and their support groups. You have seen the senior managers in your business and how relaxed they seem. They generally are friendly and genuinely concerned about what you are saying. They make a point to look you in the eye. They are able to talk with you about the health of your family and then walk into a board meeting where they face decisions that affect hundreds of thousands of employees or discuss deals where billions of dollars hang in the balance. The senior executives display a presence that has helped them achieve their position in the company. Most of them don't have ulcers, don't have heart attacks or suffer from anxiety about their company roles. They are able to separate work from their private lives and do the things that are necessary to keep them fresh and able to face new challenges as they develop. I'm not sure how much of this is learned and how much of this trait is inherent, but any insights you can learn from your senior management on how to separate work from your private life would be very helpful to you as a manager.

If you look at your area of business responsibility, and you do not see anyone having fun, then you are looking at trouble. Even during the worst times of the civil war, President Lincoln understood that he had to keep the mood light. Lincoln would tell stories to relax his cabinet and generals. When challenged about Ulysses S. Grant being a drunkard, Lincoln famously said, "Find out what whiskey he drinks and send all my generals a case, if it will get the same results."[20] Lincoln's other generals were not winning battles. In fact, Lincoln watched the Army of the Potomac sit in one place for so long that he sent a note to his general asking if he could use the army since it was obvious the general was not. Now that is getting your point across. But the point is you are responsible for the mood in your area. Your employees look to you for leadership when faced with organizational challenges. When the situation is grim, finding ways to lighten the mood and focus on what can be done reduces the stress level and is very helpful to the organization's ability to meet the challenge, whatever it might be.

In the fall of 2008, a series of bank and insurance company failures triggered a financial meltdown from which the United States and most countries are still recovering. Company sales worldwide have been impacted. Unless you oversee policy-making agencies that can change the direction of the United States' fiscal policy, you are faced with a situation you cannot change. How you handle this is how your employees will deal with it. If you run around shouting "the sky is falling, the sky is falling," then your employees will do the same. There will be no laughter, little innovation and growth. But you could make the choice to focus on what you can control, where your business is now, and figure out ways to make the business grow. By taking "the sky is falling" out of the equation, your people can be relaxed enough to think about what they CAN do under the present circumstances. This is not only healthier for your employees and the organization as a whole, but it is much more productive and can lead to ideas that will increase sales or decrease expenses. But this sometimes means you and your people need to change.

We have all heard the saying, "Laugh and the world laughs with you,"[21] but how many think of laughter as a tool to increase productivity? "Oh, we need to be very serious here; we are dealing with an important company issue affecting hundreds of people." The project may be so serious that what it really needs is a shot of light-heartedness—to relax people enough to think creatively, open up to new

55

ideas, and brainstorm. A recent WebMD article, "Give Your Body a Boost with Laughter" by R. Morgan Griffin, discusses why, for some, laughter is the best medicine. Steve Wilson, MA, CSP, psychologist and laugh therapist believes that "if people can get more laughter in their lives, they are a lot better off. They might be healthier too." Robert R. Provine, professor of psychology and neuroscience at the University of Maryland and author of *Laughter: A Scientific Investigation*, states that "Increased stress is associated with decreased immune system response."[22]

The benefits of humor and laughter are well known. "When laughter is shared, it binds people together and increases happiness and intimacy. In addition to the domino effect of joy and amusement . . . humor and laughter strengthen your immune system, boost your energy, diminish pain, and protect you from the damaging effects of stress."[23] Some studies have shown that the ability to use humor may increase infection-fighting antibodies and boost immune cells. *Readers Digest* follows this prescription with their monthly chapter "Laughter, the Best Medicine." But it's not just laughing that keeps us more productive.

Keeping your employees healthy so that they can be productive is a major challenge for some. Our aging workforce is experiencing ailments and conditions that 20 years ago people didn't think about. Some of our upcoming generations are spending less time in physical activities. This is not a good place to start when stress enters the workplace.

Add to that the changing business landscape, and it's surprising that we are achieving any forward progress at all. Before the famous US vs Russia World Chess Championship match in 1972, Bobby Fischer went to the gym to prepare. He knew that being physically fit was as important as being mentally fit. This strategy paid off for Bobby, who won the tournament against Boris Spassky, the defending champion. If physical exercise can help a chess player, then there is hope for all of us if we exercise. Many companies are now focusing on their employees' health and sponsoring initiatives to make their employees more aware of their overall health. This makes great business sense. If an employer can invest a small amount in education (teaching) they can recoup the savings in a reduction in lost time (productivity) and keep their experienced workforce focused on their jobs without them worrying about a chronic health condition. Many older workers do not know basic information such as their blood pressure, cholesterol or family health history. Then they are surprised when they suffer a heart attack or a mild stroke. Employers have a vested interest in their employees taking care of themselves. Once the employee is aware of health issues, then the harder step is to make healthy lifestyle changes. If employees are faced with lifestyle changes at home and in the workplace, this can be especially tough.

When we encounter change, just as with any new experience where the individual doesn't know what to expect, our level of anxiety rises. All individuals become anxious during change and resist it as much as possible. President Woodrow Wilson said, "If you want to make enemies, try to change something."[24] Most people dislike change. They fear change because it disrupts the way they are used to perceiving their lives. But change is unavoidable. Our whole world is constantly changing, sometimes in minor ways, such as a river gradually eroding its banks and changing the shoreline and the flow of water. Yet most companies have an unwritten saying that employees throw out when times are tough—"the only thing that doesn't change around here is that things are always changing." Making sure that change is communicated in a transparent, clear manner will help your employees understand the "What and Why" of the change. An open-door policy gives employees a chance to express their concerns before they become a block to productivity. Having a place where employees can come and feel free to speak their mind creates a less stressful environment.

It is very easy to get drawn into working 24 hours a day. Even for the most organized person, there is always something else that could be done. In the next chapter we will look at organizational tools that will help you prioritize what should be done and what could be done. It is important to differentiate between the two. Most people work so that they can have a life outside of work. But for many people work becomes their life, and the life they wanted outside of work never happens, at least not in the way they had imagined. I'm not telling you not to climb the ladder; I'm just telling you that there is a cost in doing so and that you need to use every tool available to keep your physical and emotional expenses low. Thinking of it purely in business terms, you need to maximize your return on investment (ROI) by cutting expenses where you can. Keeping your mind clear of clutter and your body sound can pay off in many ways while climbing. You are better able to separate home from work and make the real decisions when the extra effort is needed, those times where the actual payoff results in promotion or your extra effort results in increased sales or saved expenses. Putting in extra hours just to put in extra hours doesn't earn you anything and fuels your eventual burn out. Guard against this and maybe eat an apple instead of that honey bun in the employee break room vending machine. Remember what John Lennon said: "Life is what happens to you while you're busy making other plans."

CHAPTER 6

Good Management
Is Not
on Little Slips of Paper

In 1995, my boss suggested we go to a one day Time Management Seminar. I suspect the real reason he asked me to go was that he didn't want to drive by himself from Northern New Jersey to Philadelphia. I really thought that I was already organized, but when my boss offered to pay if I would drive, I agreed to go. The seminar was well worth the time. Receiving my planner at the end of the class seemed like a rite of passage, complete with a little graduation ceremony. I traveled back to New Jersey with a renewed sense of purpose, feeling I could be the poster child for organization. My job was assistant general manager for a big box retailer, and I usually worked weekends. As my boss and I returned from the seminar, he asked me to switch days off, work Friday and then take the weekend off. With the exception of the other assistant, no one else knew I was doing this. On Friday I used one of the organizational techniques I had learned the day before and cleared my desk and my in-box. I gave files to those who needed them; I handed out papers I had been keeping with notes on them and sent e-mails to managers with follow-up issues for the weekend. Since I was one of those managers whose desk and in-box usually looked like the bottom of a hamster cage, this turned out to be quite a shock for my managers and supervisors when over the weekend they saw the clean desk. They were also shocked that they received all the files and other correspondence I had been meaning to send them. By the time I arrived for work on Monday, there was a serious rumor going around that the company had transferred me, and I was no longer working in that building. At this point I became a believer in the power of planning and organization—I got everyone's attention that weekend. And I must say that I can tell, even 15 years later, how on top of my game I am by measuring the depth of my in-box.

Are there benefits to time management and organizing your day? I'd certainly say so. For example, the other morning when my alarm clock rang, I ignored the first alarm and hit the snooze button so many times it got a complex. It took forever to find my car keys; then the bagel shop was out of poppy seed and I had to settle for sesame. I told the clerk behind the counter I wanted the bagel toasted, but when I arrived at work and opened the wrapper not only was it not toasted but they had put salmon-flavored cream cheese on it, and I had asked for light butter. Next I had misplaced the code for my 10 a.m. conference call and was five minutes late logging in because I had to text a co-worker for the sign-in information. At lunch time I realized I had left my brown bag with my tuna fish sandwich and yogurt on the trunk next to the front door. This was more than a little depressing because the last time I did that my dog discovered the bag and spread the yogurt all over the living room. He didn't even bother to use the napkin I had packed. After lunch, I had a meeting with my boss to discuss the details of an upcoming project. I had assigned much of the work to one of my department managers, but because I hadn't written myself a note in my planner to remind her of the meeting, she had not brought the files in from home. So that didn't go well, and then there was the late afternoon call from a client who needed to know the status of an order. The note wasn't on my bulletin board where I usually put follow-up messages because I had taken it down to call the same client yesterday and had not put the note back. So much for a place for everything, and everything in its place! I had to call the client back, but by the time I found the information, he had left for the day. I ended up apologizing and leaving the information on his answering machine. Now I must call him again tomorrow to confirm that he received the information. Finally the work day was over, and I was *really* ready to go home. I walked out to the parking lot only to realize that I had left in such a hurry that my jacket was still on the back of the door with my car keys in the pocket. All these things are avoidable with just a little planning. You might still forget your keys, but not having a plan for keeping track of your job responsibilities is a recipe for lost productivity and much frustration.

Most management jobs require a lot of follow-up. As I mentioned before, this is one of the most challenging aspects of management. It's easy to say "Susie, take this safety training worksheet, cover it with all the 42 employees who report to you and turn in the completed worksheet to human resources before next Friday." Sounds simple. Susie says OK, and you feel that a great burden has been lifted from your shoulders. What Susie forgot was that she will be in a conference in Tucson Arizona, Monday through Wednesday, and her assistant will be taking the week off since Susie doesn't need her at the conference and the office would be slow. So what happens? Three weeks from now you get a call from the company boss at human resources. Apparently, out of over 4,000 employees, your 42 employees were the only ones in the entire company who did not receive the safety training. Ouch. So off you go to yell at Susie, but you really should stay in your office and yell in the mirror. Not following up happens all the time. It may not be a big training project—maybe you forgot to schedule an employee's day off, or you didn't call a client about the release of your new product. If you don't have a system for remembering priorities, your client may become someone else's client, and the sale is lost to your competition.

Having the right information at your fingertips is generally the sign of an organized individual. I don't try to remember everything, but I always try to remember where to get certain information. I may not know all the individual steps for a specific task, but give me 30 seconds and I can print out or retrieve the entire 17 page step-by-step instructions. I tell people my knowledge is two miles wide and two inches deep. Having a plan for what you keep and what you put away helps in the organizational process. Most of us are envious of the co-worker who has the clean desk and the files with color-coordinated labels, all typed in the same font. But not many of us are willing to put in the effort necessary to maintain such a system. But don't feel badly if your system is not neat. You do not have to be neat to be organized. Although there are benefits to being neat, neat does not always mean organized. My personal style is part hamster cage shredded paper. That's my in-box where I put everything that I want available but don't want to file because then I will never get around to working on it. The other part of my system is organized file folders, without the color coordinated tabs. I keep monthly records with everything pertaining to that month in a folder. Then next year, when I pull out last year to do my budgeting for this year, I have all my information in one place.

Cassandra R. Lee, a self-development expert and corporate trainer, posted an Ezine article on "Organizational Techniques—4 Ways to Elevate Your Efficiency"[25] in your workplace or business environment as follows:

#1 File to Find Information Quickly—I have folders set up for recurring reports. When they arrive in my in-box, I review them at once and then open the file drawer and place them in the folder. DONE! If I need to review them later, I know where they are.

#2 Use a 31-day Tickler File—I have used this in the past with monthly deadlines and it does work. Now that my computer gives me access to great calendar tools, my 31-day tickler is attached to my e-mail, and any deadlines pop up as a reminder. For very important events, I set an early warning reminder that the true deadline is coming.

#3 Work from a Clean Desk—there is a certain peace that sets in when you start a job if you can lay it out on an empty desk. When you have to shove piles of papers onto the corner of your desk to have a place to work, your mind is unconsciously distracted by the piles of papers. You are working on a report due this afternoon, but your subconscious is working through the paper clutter in front of you while you are trying to solve these issues. You are not able to focus on the present task. I find it helpful to either clear my desk or head to the conference room and use the empty table there. I can think more clearly when there are no distractions.

#4 Complete Most Important Task First—I have seen this illustrated in many different ways over the years. I once did an employee meeting on prioritizing. I spread out poker chips on a table using red, white and blue chips. I explained the value of each chip, and then I had each employee come up and chose a chip. Since the blue were more valuable, every employee chose a blue chip. I then linked their choosing the most valuable chip with choosing the most important task to work on each day. I asked them to carry the blue chip in their pocket to remind themselves to focus on the most important task first.

You can pay for seminars from leading day planner companies, and they will teach you these same techniques. Remember, I am not teaching you anything new. This didn't just come to me in the shower. These ideas and techniques have been successfully used by people long before I sat down at the keyboard to write. Once again, this makes it very exciting because there is information out there that will help make you more successful. You don't have to invent a new system. You can piggyback on what's already available and add your own personal touch. The day planner that I use has a specific coding system for prioritizing tasks. The system you use is not what is important, but that you use a system. No excuses about why you are not organized; just get started. Research shows that it takes 21 consecutive days to establish a new a habit. By the end of the first month, if you have committed to using a set of organizational techniques you will find that they become second nature. If you miss a day of planning and writing in your day planner, you will feel it and be prompted to get back on track. Weight loss, smoking cessation and other life-changing programs all rely on this human nature. As you look at the different tools available to you, think about what will be easiest for you to use and then get started. Set aside time to organize your files, clean your desk and then make it your goal to do the most important tasks first. It might be more fun to make some phone calls or look at your e-mail, but if you have marked completing the 2011 departmental budget proposal as your most important task, do that first. Then look at your planner and choose the task you marked as the second most important.

I am not selling a specific system, but I would recommend that everyone use something more formal than the back of an envelope. I have used that and it doesn't work in the long run. I have worked with and managed people who use the "I don't have to write this down because I remember everything" technique. I wasn't that bold to think I could remember everything, so I used the little slips of paper method from time to time. The biggest change I saw when I started using a day planner was that I dispensed with all my little slips of paper. I have one place for my notes. When I do not have my planner and I'm writing on a napkin or the back of a business card or a piece of a box, I carry the handwritten note around until I can transfer it to my planner. Then I throw the piece of paper away. I know that if I put a note in my pocket, I will eventually find it, but the deadline may have passed. Discipline yourself to keep one list; toss the little slips away after you have entered them into your planner, and you will be on your way to being enjoyably organized.

CHAPTER 7

Good Management
Is Not
Hiring a Pulse

What I have learned from 30 years of interviewing potential employees is that many people know nothing about the company that is interviewing them. They are not able to tell the prospective employer, me, how they would benefit the company. They do not, or seemingly cannot even when prompted, state examples of how they have 1. increased sales, 2. decreased costs, 3. improved productivity, or 4. handled customer service issues successfully. They do not give specific examples of what they have achieved. They do not dress for the interview, show up on time, have a firm handshake, or look me in the eye. Many interviewees don't seem enthusiastic about being there in the first place. Young people and even some older adults show up as if their mommies had dressed them up and sent them out saying,

"Don't come back until you find a job." They show no sense of ownership about the process and no follow-up after the interview is completed.

Being open-minded, I always try to give the applicant a chance to shine. In fact, as part of the icebreaking introduction, I remind them that they will have an opportunity to show off what they have done and to let me know why I should choose them out of all the applicants I will see that day. But many times, even when reminded during the interview process, they will not or cannot think of anything. Sometimes as I listen to an applicant, I find that I am humming to myself a tune from the Grasshopper and the Ants (a Walt Disney cartoon based on an Aesop fable) where the grasshopper sings, "Oh, the world owes me a livin'!" But wait, you might say, I NEED PEOPLE NOW! I HAVE A PROJECT DUE NEXT WEEK, AND I AM UNDERSTAFFED!

I can honestly say that I have felt like that at times over the years, and I'm sure that I've let managers hire less than stellar applicants. But more recently when interviewing potential applicants, I have resisted the temptation to just say "breath onto this mirror." Actually taking the time to find the right person does create more work. But having the right people in the end makes the effort worthwhile. Last fall I knew of a store that screened 116 applicants for seasonal positions over a two-week period. Eighteen didn't make it past the telephone interview; eight didn't show up at all for their interviews, and of the remaining 90, they hired 32. That's comparable to the effort needed to drive to the seafood market, purchase several hundred bushels of oysters, drive home and drag the bushels of oysters around to the picnic table in the back yard. Then you would need to go inside and get your oyster shucking knife from the kitchen drawer, return to the picnic table, dump the bushels of oysters on the table and begin shucking them. If you have not shucked an oyster, the trick is to get the knife blade in between the two shell halves just in front of the muscle. Then you can apply a little sideways pressure to the knife blade and the shell will begin to open. When you interview you are trying to get the applicant to open up, just like an oyster, to see what is inside. Your goal is to find the pearl in the pile of ordinary oysters. So to hire 32 pearls, or great employees, you would need to shuck at least 116 oysters, or applicants. What work! But the effort paid off for this store with a better group of seasonal employees than they had hired the previous year.

Hiring the right way and not just "hiring a pulse" can be a lot of work. Not only must you invest the manager's time to do the interview, but you also have to pay their salaries. Then you must pay someone to process the paperwork, conduct drug tests and background checks (if that is your policy) and record where each applicant is in the hiring process. On average, the total cost of hiring an entry level staff manager with less than three years experience is $9,777.

Hiring someone with three or more years experience can cost $19, 219, and the cost of hiring at the executive level can be $30,277. Make the right decisions with the right tools can save your company big chunks of money. But make the wrong decision and have to start over costs even more than the figures quoted above. Lost productivity is everywhere when you hire the wrong person. Management has to focus on correcting the problem instead of driving sales or cutting expenses. The employees in the company know something is going on with the new hire and possibly they are talking about it, which drains productivity, or they are picking up the slack, which drains morale, or perhaps they are still upset that you hired someone who knows less about the company than they do and is now their boss.

I remember interviewing this one fellow. The building was a storefront we had rented, with large picture windows in the front. As I reviewed the applicant's resume and work history, my fellow manager brought the potential employee to my desk. I was impressed by his work history in companies similar to ours. He had been promoted in one job and had left each job only to advance his career. Each of the three companies he had worked for provided good recommendations. His current employer could only offer him part-time hours and no benefits. He was looking for a full-time position with benefits. I was really excited about interviewing this person. Then I actually met him.

James (not his real name) was dressed in a long-sleeved white shirt with a plaid tie, khaki pants and dress shoes. He looked professional as he approached the desk. And then he put out his hand. There was no enthusiasm as he shook my hand. I introduced myself and thanked him for coming. He mumbled, "Sure." I asked him to have a seat and tried to put him at ease. I explained the interview process and encouraged him to give me examples of what he had done in his previous jobs that would benefit our company. He thought that would be a good idea, but he never did. In fact, he was very reserved—getting any answers from him was like pulling teeth.

As the interview progressed and I was not getting any examples of how he had saved his previous employers money, increased sales, or solved problems, I tried to give him the answers with statements such as "I see you worked for Acme for two years and were promoted twice. Tell me how you did that?" Nothing. "I see you were with Academy Sales and your division received your company's top award last year. What did you do to make that possible?" Nothing. "In college, you were on the Dean's list and worked a part-time job on campus. How did you organize your time to be successful in both areas?" Nothing.

I know you are not supposed to give the answers away when you ask the question, but I was sure if I could get him thinking about what had made him successful in his prior jobs he could tell me how he would benefit my company.

Still nothing. It was frustrating and a little sad because I could see in his eyes that there was not really anything going on inside his head when I asked him questions. Mostly a blank stare and a few crumbs of a response. I finally told him I was interviewing many applicants today and that I would forward his information to our HR department for further consideration. I thanked him for his time, and he walked out into the street.

Moments later I saw him standing on the street corner talking to someone on his cell phone. His face was animated, and I could see that he was very interested in the conversation. He even began to gesture with the hand not holding the phone. As I watched him through the window, I thought to myself if he had put that much energy into his interview, I would have hired him. He clearly could get excited and enthusiastic about some things, but not about this job. Part of me thought I had failed because I could not get him to open up, but mostly I believed I had made the right hiring decision. In spite of his impressive resume, he could not "talk the talk and walk the walk." This was my first meeting with James, and I expected that he would be on his best behavior. If this was all I could get from him when it mattered the most, what could I expect if I actually hired him? I believed I would find him excited only about what he wanted to do. I spent 45 minutes trying to prove my first impression wrong because of his impressive resume, but in the end, I went with my gut feeling.

Interestingly, most of the good applicants stood out from the moment they sat down. Somehow as managers we get a gut feeling that we apply to the hiring process. That feeling is not the desperate feeling I NEED PEOPLE NOW! That feeling is the enthusiasm and interest in the position that comes through when you are talking to someone who gets it. They are able to cite specific examples; they are engaged and pay attention to what you are talking about. They ask questions and want to know more. They want to know when you will make a decision and follow-up with a phone call after the interview. By asking the right questions and getting specific examples, you can separate the person who gets it from the candidate who is just blowing smoke. Some people know how to interview and always seem to have the right answers. But something about them raises a red flag. The more they talk, the more you begin to feel that they are just telling you what you want to hear. If you are interviewing from an I NEED PEOPLE NOW mindset, you may miss the fact that they are giving you examples of only what they expect you want to hear. They are not necessarily giving you examples of things they have actually done or are likely to do if hired. To use the vernacular—they give a good interview. If hired, these applicants are the first ones who suddenly remember that they really can't work Fridays and Aunt Betsy is coming on the 17th, so they can't work after 3 p.m. that day. They go from open availability to the world owes me a living. This transformation usually occurs just after the probationary period ends. Once the threat of immediate termination is taken off the table by permanent status, the wrong new hires now are the wrong employees. They require extra attention that takes energy away from focusing on things like driving sales and reducing costs. Longer term employees resent them or worse, they begin to follow their lead and performance suffers.

If you haven't read *Blink: The Power of Thinking Without Thinking* by Malcolm Gladwell, I highly recommend it. He attempts to explain how our brains generate insights from thin slices of information. He tells the story of a fire chief putting out a kitchen fire inside a single family home with a basement. His crew had knocked down the fire twice, but it came back very quickly. As his men were doing this for the third time, he sensed that the fire was not acting properly, that something was fundamentally wrong. He ordered his crew out of the house at once. As they backed out of the living room onto the front porch, the entire floor where they had just been standing collapsed fully engulfed in flames. The gut feeling of that fire chief saved the lives of himself and his crew.

That same gut feeling combined with the SMART[26] method of checking objectives (specific, measurable, achievable, realistic, and time-based) can be a great tool in selecting the right applicant. Your initial impression is usually correct. Ask the right questions, and if the applicant responds with examples of actual success stories you can decide if your gut feeling is correct. To avoid hiring mistakes, two or more different managers should interview the applicant. If the applicant is putting on a show and knows the right answers to get hired, this will most likely appear in the second or final interview. The interview process should be designed to find out about the candidate first, and then sell him or her on your company. Giving out too much information about the company and what you are looking for is giving the applicant the answers to the test. The applicant has heard you say you are looking for a system analyst who is fluent in fourth generation languages (4GL) and object-orientated programming. Now they are suddenly versed in this area even if their exposure to either subject was a two-hour seminar put on by a vendor who wanted their previous firm's business. By giving away the answers, you have made hiring the right candidate harder. However, all is not lost because a second and third interview will often catch discrepancies in work history, job responsibilities and attitude. Good candidates with solid job histories will be consistent in any series of interviews with good examples of how they have increased sales or reduced expenses. They will display a consistent, positive attitude and will leave the interview only after confirming what the next step in the process is for them. Now, this seems like a lot of work on your part. Arranging up to three interviews with different members of your staff can take away from your day-to-day responsibilities. But by taking the time to avoid hiring the wrong candidate, you will save time and energy in the future. If you can't afford to be selective now, you will suffer the long-term consequences, possibly for years to come. As Harvey Firestone said, "When people think of business as a mere matter of merchandise, of buying and selling goods, they overlook what is perhaps the most important, and certainly the most interesting, factor in the game. It takes men to produce merchandise. It takes men to sell it. To get the right kind of men is, therefore, the chief concern of every executive."[27]

Many managers see hiring as taking time away from their real responsibilities. They don't realize that by just hiring a pulse and not investing the time necessary to make an informed decision about an individual, they are creating the problems they will be complaining about eight to ten months down the road. You will hear the manager who did a sloppy job interviewing say, "How did this employee make it past probation?" They forget that they hired this employee in the first place and are responsible for them being part of the company. The fact that this manager didn't give effective feedback about the new hire's performance during the probationary period has now saddled the company with a marginal employee who is dragging down productivity. The new hire has not taken ownership of their position just as the manager who hired them did not take ownership of the hiring process. Either way, the road ahead is long and bumpy and usually ends with a conference call that includes the former employee, the manager who eventually fired the employee, and the labor board advocate who is determining if the former employee is entitled to unemployment benefits. All this is because the manager did not take the hiring process seriously.

Andrew Carnegie said of his best hires, "You will never be a partner unless you know the business of your department far better than the owners possibly can. When called to account for your independent action, show him the result of your genius, and tell him that you knew it would be so; show him how mistaken the orders were. . . . Some of them have acted upon occasion with me as if they owned the firm and I was but some airy New Yorker presuming to advise upon what I knew very little about. Well, they are not interfered with much now. They were the true bosses—the very men we were looking for."[28]

When you find a candidate that exhibits the characteristics found in Andrew Carnegie's quote, hire them on the spot. Your challenge when hiring is to take the time to find and recognize talent—people with the skills that your company needs. To recognize individuals with a proven record of accomplishment, an individual who has increased sales, decreased expenses, improved customer service and can give you examples of how this was done. These candidates are your best chance to hire the best employee because they are already doing what you need done. Right now they are just doing it for someone else. Their previous actions are the best predictor of future behavior, and those that can demonstrate the skills you are looking for will almost always produce the same positive results or better in a new environment.

CHAPTER 8

Good Management

Is Not

a 10

Honest appraisals begin the day you hire someone. If you are not giving your employees honest feedback each time you interact, they may well be blindsided when they receive their annual evaluation. Or, just as bad, and many times worse, they will not get any feedback during the year, and their review will reflect average performance. Yet you feel there is something that is keeping them from moving ahead. By not being honest with them, they don't know what you want them to improve. So how can they fix it, if they don't know?

The SMART goals method developed by Peter Drucker in 1954, provided managers with a method to formalize the review process. Goals became specific, measurable, attainable, realistic and timely. Now managers had a way to measure performance, and employees were given clear expectations, not subjective and undefined goals such as "secure more contracts for the company." A smart goal would be "in the fiscal year 2010, increase signed contracts 7% over the fiscal year 2009." Or instead of "don't spend as much this year on equipment," would be "decrease equipment expenditure this year by 10% to 1.26 million vs 1.40 million last year."

You can also be more specific when discussing employee training. "Have two area supervisors recommended for promotion by the 3rd quarter of our new fiscal year." The idea is to make the goal clear enough that the person working to achieve the goal understands what the goal is, and equally as important the person measuring the goal knows if the goal was met. In spite of the great interest in SMART goals (15,900,000 hits on Google), few managers in my day-to-day experience apply it to their daily work.

I can't tell you how many reviews I have read that are so vague that you wonder what the employee is really being asked to do. For example, a goal for next year could be "Sally, improve productivity." What does that mean? OK, she is an engineer for a jet manufacturing firm, so we assume she is being told to make changes in the way she works on her specific project, but even that is not clear when you just tell someone to "improve productivity." Besides, shouldn't Sally know what I mean? After all it's her project. But what if the manager said, "Sally, by the end of the next fiscal year, your division must reduce cost overruns on the A-40 turbine engine by 15 basis points over last year?" That's a little more specific. It's not just "improve productivity" but how to work more productively on her project. Now Sally knows where you want her to focus. Being specific is very important to the employee's success and to your area. Sally may have been thinking, make the engine faster when you gave her the goal to improve productivity. If you are vague, Sally walks away from the review focused on something that may require additional resources and will actually increase cost overruns, creating exactly the opposite result you were looking for.

Following Sally's review, her manager needs to tell her how she can know if she is meeting the job expectations. She can look at the costs and know right away that her project is actually three basis points below last year in cost overruns. She can track the results on a quarter by quarter basis against last year and see her progress. When Sally's manager decided that her goal should be reducing cost overruns on the A-40 turbine engine by 15 basis points over last year, he may have looked at the industry, the competition and the performance of other divisions of his own company and found that others are achieving similar results. Therefore, to challenge Sally to produce the same results is both attainable and realistic. But what if her manager had asked her to spend 50% less than last year and make the A-40 turbine engine run at warp drive, similar to the Star Trek propulsion system of the fictional Starship Enterprise? This is clearly not realistic, regardless of how much fun that would be if it actually worked. The final objective is that Sally needs a time limit. What time frame are we talking about? When Sally is told to increase productivity she will work within the time frame she thinks is appropriate, or she may think that there is no time limit, and this is an ongoing project to work on whenever she can. But if her manager has said to her, "By the end of the next fiscal year," then he has given her a measureable goal and a time for completion. Sally can put the end date on a calendar and work backwards to see how she is performing towards that goal.

I have reviewed many performance appraisals given by managers over the years, and there are several camps of thought. One says, "Nobody is excellent; there is always something to work on. I never give anyone an excellent rating for anything! If they are performing above expectations, isn't that really their job? Why should I give them an excellent rating for doing their job?" These same managers will likely go the other way and say, "There are things that need to be worked on," so they rate the employee 'needs improvement', instead of 'satisfactory.' Now you have a good employee who is told in their review that they are only meeting expectations and need improvement in several areas. And yet, they were the one employee who saved the Parker account because they were methodical and organized and recognized an error in the bid that would have cost the company millions of dollars in lost profit. How will this employee feel motivated to perform at a higher level if they are only told that they meet expectations, although they know that they single-handedly saved the company millions? This happens when a manager's style keeps him or her from giving adequate praise when it is due. If the employee is not recognized and rewarded with enough positive feedback for protecting the company's bottom line, the end result may be that this manager will push the employee to find a company that recognizes their positive contributions. So now this manager has created a void that must be filled, and the time and expense necessary to replace an employee is paid by the company. In the meantime, the former employee's fellow workers pick up the slack, which can lead to morale issues, or create a void that another employee will have to fill. However, once this employee begins to contribute at a higher level and is not recognized for their contribution, the process repeats itself.

Then there are those managers who fear the review process. They don't want to make waves with their employees, and so the review process becomes a non-threatening but unrealistic review of the employee's performance. Jeremy was a strongly opinionated employee. Jeremy was always gossiping. And he had this habit of calling in sick around major holidays. In fact, he was so consistent that managers would take bets as to how many days before Christmas he would begin his annual problem.

Jeremy, who wanted to be promoted into management, has not been chosen for the last two positions he applied for. He is fairly effective in the day-to-day activities of his current position, but he cannot be counted on during the crunch times. His gossiping with fellow employees often makes the whole department less productive. Many of his co-workers don't want to offend him, but they are bothered when he wants to share what happened at dinner last night, or what he saw Jeff doing. Behind his back, management cannot envision this employee becoming a manager, yet his annual reviews do not reflect any concerns. In fact, his review suggests that he should keep applying for management positions. By not being honest with an employee, the employee is baffled when they are not promoted. Similarly, management is baffled as to why the employee expects to be promoted. Yet in reality, no manager has ever sat down with this employee and honestly explained the issues. Instead they have written a 10 review for an employee they feel is a 5, maybe a 6 at best. They are afraid to address the real issue and hide behind the performance appraisal. Without giving this employee specific measurable goals, how can he address issues and become eligible for promotion?

The best performance appraisals offer no surprises and give specific measurable goals for the coming year. In fact, if the annual review is the first time an employee learns of a problem, then the manager isn't doing his or her job. If an on-going performance issue hasn't been addressed, it's not always the employee's fault that it hasn't been corrected. Yet managers often blame the employee for their inability to perform certain tasks. "I've told Brian 100 times how to do this, why can't he get it right?" Well, isn't that the definition of insanity? You do the same thing time after time but expect a different result.

Harvey Firestone knew that his employees' performance was directly linked to how he managed. If his employees got it, then he was doing his job. If they didn't, then he knew who's fault it was. "I hold that, if anything in the business is wrong, the fault is squarely with management. If the tires were not made right, if the workmen are unhappy, if the sales are not what they ought to be, the fault is not with the man who is actually doing the job, but with the men above him and the men above them, so that, finally, the fault is mine. That is my conception of business."[28]

Good managers will quickly recognize when the employee is not getting it, and they will find another way to get their message across. This may involve retraining for the particular task, using pictures instead of a printed manual, or sending the employee for specific training. In the end, getting the message across may involve corrective consultations. When the annual review comes around, the employee should recognize in the comments section that they have been coached about any performance issues. They should say "I remember when that happened, and you gave me additional training and a copy of the step by step diagrams.

That really helped me understand the job requirements." When your employee gives you feedback during a performance review, you know that you have successfully communicated your job expectations to your employee.

The best performance reviews include input from the employee and agreement on what their goals and focus areas should be for the coming year. The review should include not only areas of focus, but also recognition of areas where the employee is doing well. "Susie has increased her department sales 6.79% over fiscal year 2008 exceeding all other departments in her division by 42 basis points. Tim's work on cellular structure earned him the Science Fellows Medal and resulted in our company being awarded a $50 million grant to continue the research." But don't be afraid to recognize the everyday if that is a key element in the employee's job. Fred is a cashier for a local supermarket, and accuracy is a key element in the successful execution of his job. "During the past year Fred's till has balanced to the penny, 54 out of 55 weeks." As you are challenging them to do even more next year, make sure that you thank your employees for doing things well. I'm sure you expect someone to say "job well done" when you get your review.

Another area that needs to be addressed is how you handle internal promotions. More importantly, how do you communicate with your employees who applied for a position and then found out that you are hiring outside your department or outside the company to find the right candidate? When you advertise a position that you are not going to promote from within, you should be aware of the impact on your current employees. You are going outside for a reason. Make sure that your employees know where they stand. If you have given them honest feedback during their annual review, there should be no surprises. If you have interviewed your employees, and none of them meet the requirements, then it is important for you to share with them why they did not get the job. By being honest and giving them specific examples of where they need to improve to be considered the next time, you are helping your employees to grow. You are also placing the responsibility on them by giving them the tools they need to be successful and the opportunity to correct issues that you believe are holding them back. Anything less and you will create ill will and productivity will suffer.

Giving honest, daily feedback is one of the traits of a successful manager. After all, how do your employees know they need to change if you do not tell them? By talking with them, your employees will know what they need to do to secure that next promotion when the time comes. By taking that worry off their minds, they can better focus on their daily jobs. They will be more creative because they know you are behind them. They receive the praise they deserve when things are going well and the feedback they need to help them continue to grow. As their manager, you enjoy the esoteric satisfaction of helping another person achieve his or her goals. But basically, you get a productive employee you can count on when the going gets tough—one who will make the same decisions you would. And that makes your job so much easier.

CHAPTER 9

Good Management
Is Not
Leadership

"Leaders inspire people with clear visions of how things can be done better"[29] said Jack Welch, former CEO of General Electric. The problem with being a leader and focusing on the big picture is that you can't be too concerned with the details. But that is what most managers are expected to do. They must manage and administer programs and policies, many of which they had no part in creating. Managing these programs requires attention to detail. Details are not really a leadership function; they are a managerial function. For instance, you must sign your time card to confirm that it is accurate before you can pick up your paycheck. If the employee's manager doesn't review the time cards before handing out the paychecks, he can be in violation of company attendance policy, if they have this policy. Employees usually are allowed to miss a specific number of days before they receive counseling notices about their continued absences. If one department manager is reviewing this daily and another hasn't looked at an employee's punches in months, there can be problems. And not just for the manager who is not paying attention, but the entire company can be liable for the manager being negligent.

If you are spending all your time on long-range planning, who is minding the store? Who is teaching your employees their job responsibilities? Who is holding them accountable for their actions when they produce less than what is expected? And who is praising those that are clearly exceeding expectations? If you are glossing over the details, you are not managing your business.

Warren Bennis and Burt Nanus on the cover of their book *Leaders* quote Peter Drucker: "Management is doing things right; leadership is doing the right things." That's a catchy phrase, and people use it so often that it must be true. However, the nuts and bolts of it are more basic. The two sayings are very much the same but also entirely different. As a manager, I make sure that the details are taken care of. As a leader, I must plan for the near future. But my title is manager and that means I am responsible for managing the details. Did the weekly payroll get closed out? Did every department turn in their safety training, and have the facility audit issues recorded by our internal auditor been resolved?

Even though I think of myself as a leader, I am also a clerk, checking off my list, making sure that the details are taken care of in a timely manner. Not very glamorous really, but it is the basis of my job. Without someone focusing on executing the day-to-day business activities, there would be no need for any long-term planning and leadership. There would be no one to lead because without focus on the basics, there would be no business. If no one answered the phone one day at your company, how much business would you lose? As the manager, I am charged with making sure that activity is covered. If I'm too busy brainstorming and planning future events to notice that the person in charge of answering the phones didn't come in, that's a problem. If I don't approve the time cards and the employees don't get paid on Friday, that's a problem. And if the front door to the office building is locked during normal business hours, or the person who responds to e-mail requests for sales information calls out and I don't replace them, that's a problem. Almost all these activities are not specifically addressed in my job description, but they appear under the innocuous heading of "miscellaneous other." These are management functions. You are managing your business when you complete these tasks. You are not leading when you do these tasks, but they are part of your job. You can probably think of 10 to 20 miscellaneous other tasks that you complete everyday in your job. This is not the stuff that will necessarily get you promoted, yet not doing it will certainly get you noticed, but not for the right reasons. But all is not lost.

If you manage effectively, you end up being a leader. Herbert Casson said about leadership "As soon as a man climbs up to a high position, he must train his subordinates and trust them. They must relieve him of all small matters. He must be set free to think, to travel, to plan, to see important customers, to make improvements, to do all the big jobs of leadership."[30] So now we are back to teaching. I mentioned at the beginning that my intention was not to reinvent management, but to remind you of what you already knew and what was important. Well, I am reminding you now that a large part of your job is teaching. You teach your employees to alert you if the person who answers the phone is calling out for the day. Then you can react and find a substitute, or even better, you teach your supervisors what to do with employee call outs. Instead of passing by the receptionist's desk an hour after you have opened only to find out no one is there, you actually get a call from one of your supervisors 15 minutes before you open saying, "Oh, by the way, April called out today, but I asked James to come in. He will be here by 10:30 and in the meantime, Anne from accounting is taking care of the phones." Problem solved. And all you had to do was empower your management team to make decisions. You had to invest some of your time in teaching, and now you are free to focus on other activities such as driving sales and reducing expenses.

What is leadership? As defined by Dictionary.com, leadership is 1. the position or function of a leader. 2. ability to lead. 3. an act or instance of leading; guidance; direction. 4. the leaders of a group.[31] None of this seems very helpful in identifying what makes a leader other than being able to lead. It is generally assumed that the leader would be leading more than just him or herself, but one can picture doing it alone.

Recently, Phil Mickelson, currently ranked the second best golf player in the world, talked about becoming the number one golfer. Phil correctly pointed out in an interview before the US Open at Pebble Beach, CA that his job was to play each shot well. If he followed his course management and updated his plan daily based upon course conditions, he would put himself in a position to win the US Open. If he did that, he'd replace Tiger Woods as the Number 1 golfer in the world. Not a bad title to have. So Phil was not thinking at all about the title, but he was thinking about each shot, each small decision that he had to make on the course. He knew that if he did that correctly, the title will logically follow. In fact, the most successful people, the ones who make serious money (as one measure of success) or become the #1 golfer in the world are focused not on making money or the title but on being the best they can in their chosen profession. The money and title follow when you are the best, not the other way around. I therefore submit that being the best manager you can be will make you a great leader. Failure to understand your job and the management functions will keep you from being a good manager and derail your plans to be a great leader.

In an emergency, it's easy to lead. "Follow me the building is on fire, and I know the way to the only safe exit." The people that don't follow you will end up as part of Darwin's natural selection process. Everyone else will be eternally grateful to you; heck, they may even throw you a parade and pin a medal on you at a town meeting. But what about the day-to-day encounters with your employees? How do you convince them to follow you with the same enthusiasm that they would if you were saving their lives? What do you need to do to have the Parker account on your desk by noon tomorrow or 40 containers of sale merchandise through customs and into your stores before your grand opening? Leading your employees to the goal requires the use of management tools, planning and coordination, and an ability to focus on the small details so that the big picture can be achieved. When all this works together and your employees follow your lead in focusing on the process, the result can be that you have led your team to a successful grand opening, negotiated the customs hurdle and the product arrived at your locations in time for the grand opening. Yes, you did lead your team, but you didn't accomplish this by leading. You did it by managing.

In a previous chapter I talked about checklists. Management is performing a series of checklists to insure that the end result is achieved. These checklists may not even be written down. Much of what I do I have done every day for 30 years or more. Yet, I am still more effective when I use a checklist, which helps me keep the most important items in focus. As a manager, I must check on my employees and follow up on their progress to make sure that the business objectives are met and that my employees perform all the day-to-day tasks that make the business successful. It is not enough for me to stand at a podium with the company flag blown up on the wall behind me and say, "Ok team, make me proud" and walk off the stage smoking a pipe and wearing the company banner over my shoulder. My job as a manager is to be in the trenches with the employees, reviewing their progress, checking on the results they obtain and making adjustments as needed. In the end I probably led them to a successful conclusion, but I didn't do it by leading. I did it by managing. By teaching, observing and following up, you can be a successful manager and at the same time be recognized as a leader.

CHAPTER 10

Final Thoughts

Thirty-five years ago, as a gas station manager with a staff of eight employees, I experienced my first management lesson about employee theft. I had learned to do a schedule and deal with customers, but this was a hugely different problem. At the time of the oil incident, company policy never entered my mind. What he did was just wrong, and I knew it was wrong. I didn't need a company manual to tell me. I'm not even sure that there was a company manual. We were a small regional gas chain, with 30 locations in the Tidewater Virginia area. There was no employee handbook, no book of standard operating procedures. But I didn't need that to know what to do; I had learned right from wrong when I was seven. My Mother had taken me and my friend Kyle, who lived down the street, to the Red Door Country Store. We both had a few pennies for candy. While I was looking at the candy, Kyle walked away. Soon he was brought back to where my mother and I were standing by the owner who had seen him put candy in his pockets. The owner was yelling at him that he was stealing. At seven that was quite a shock. Since then I have never wanted to have an experience like that. Back to Scott and the oil incident, I told Scott I would have to fire him if he ever did anything like that again. I reminded him that I had hired him because he was the brother of one of my best friends in high school and that I knew his mother. I never saw him do it again, but he soon found a different job and left the gas station.

Having your employees get it may be as simple as telling them a story. When Don Hewitt, the creator and executive producer of *60 Minutes* (one of the longest running shows in U.S. television history) died at age 86, John Baldoni wrote an article about Hewitt titled "Why Leaders need Stories." Don Hewiit explained his secret of success this way. "Even the people who wrote the Bible were smart enough to know, 'tell them a story.' The issue was evil in the world, the story was Noah.... Now the Bible knew that and for some reason or another I latched on to that."[32]

I have been talking in each chapter about ways you can make your employees "get your message" and be more productive, more focused on the company goals and make your job easier in the end. I have included many stories in this book. As John Baldoni wrote, "a good story can be a useful leadership tool to inform, involve and inspire."[32] You can do the same with your employees. If you have not been around long enough to have stories, then you can search the web, or do it the old-fashioned way and read *Forbes Book of*

Business Quotations. I suspect that if each of you reflected for a few minutes, you could think of several stories to illustrate a point you were trying to make to your staff.

I have talked a lot about employees and your responsibility to them. Michael Quinlan, President of McDonald's Corporation said that "one of the most important aspects of his job—and one at which he spends approximately one-third of his time—was cutting red tape"[33] Everything I have talked about relates to making sure you are doing the right thing for your employees. Sometimes they need guidance, direction, even the possibility of written documentation or loss of pay. But sometimes, they just need you to clear the way so they can do what you hired them to do. The whole reason you have employees in the first place is because your business is too big to be operated by yourself. That is a good thing. But to make the most of your employees they have to move effectively and efficiently through the company paperwork and reporting requirements. They need your support when another part of the company is not willing to help. These employees forget that they are on the same team and that they are really helping the company succeed when they help another division within the same company. Unfortunately, many managers become territorial and think first and foremost about covering their own area. Your job then is to ensure that your employees receive the support and tools they need to do their job.

When considering how to apply what you have read, think about what Queen Elizabeth II said on this subject. "It's all to do with the training: you can do a lot if you are properly trained."[34] Managing a kingdom is like running a multi-national corporation, a mom and pop store or a department within a larger company. You are constantly fending off rival kingdoms (competitors); you have to keep your subjects (employees) in line, either by rewarding them or punishing them, and you have to stay in power (profitable) to reap the benefits. In the 1600s, King Charles I failed to get the City (London) to expand its boundaries to include new populations. He was beheaded in 1649. Not all modern day leaders are successful either. CEO's have been removed, like Dick Grasso who was ousted as chairman and chief executive of the New York Stock Exchange in 2003. But John Thain, the ex-CEO of Merrill Lynch, who once held top posts at Goldman Sachs and the New York Stock Exchange, was removed and then returned in 2010 as chairman and CEO of the Commercial Investment Trust (CIT Group, Inc.). One fended off the attacks and reinvented himself; he had found a group that "got" what he was doing. The other one was not able to defend his position and was forced to withdraw. The opposition had brought in reinforcements and in the end he was the one who got it.

The same rules apply especially if you are not the CEO. Your success as a manager and your ability to be promoted, to take on additional responsibility in your organization, with the additional compensation that goes with it, depends on your ability to draw the most from your employees. If you can teach them how to do their jobs the same way you would do it, you will be successful. Dr. Joseph Collins said, "A prudent person profits from personal experience, a wise one from the experience of others."[35] I am asking you to think and feel what you already know, to use common sense, to be wise, and when you do that to have the courage to act upon it. I hope you will close this book thinking, "He spoke for a lot of us. And he just reinforced what we already knew."

Notes

1. Gomez-Mejia, Luis R., Balkin, David B., & Cardy, Robert L. (2008). *Management: People, Performance, Change, 3rd edition.* New York, New York USA: McGraw-Hill, p. 19.

2. Smith, George David, & Dalzell, Frederick. (2000). *Wisdom from the Robber Barons: Enduring Business Lessons from Rockefeller, Morgan, and the First Industrialists. New York. New York USA: Basic Books, p. 42.*

3. Barrett, Richard. (2003). *Vocational Business: Training, Developing and Motivating People.* Cheltenham UK: Nelson Thornes, p. 51.

4. Iacocca, Lee. Lee Iacocca quote: "Management is nothing more than motivating other people." Retrieved April 2, 2010 from http://www.quotes.net/quote/4

5. Retrieved August 7, 2010 from http://www.pithypedia.com/?similarquotes...a...

6. Coonley, Howard. "Howard Coonley: Thoughts and Quotes." Retrieved August 11, 2010 from http://thoughts.forbes.com/thoughts/howard-coonley

7. Metzman, Gustav. "A Collection of Thoughts, Quotes and Sayings" by Gustav Metzman. Retrieved August 9, 2010 from http://thoughts.forbes.com/thoughts/gustav-metzman

8. Italics (author).

9. Encyclopedia of Business and Finance. "Labor Unions." Retrieved September 3, 2010, from http://:www.enotes.com

10. Boone, Louis E., & Kurtz, David L. (1999). *Contemporary Business.* Fort Worth, TX: Dryden Press, p. 414.

11. "Welch's Seven-Point Program for Management by Leadership."
    Retrieved June 7, 2010, from
    http://www.1000ventures.com/business_guide/crosscuttings/cs_lead
    ership_welch.html

12. Burton, Katherine, & Effinger, Anthony. (Feb 26, 2010). "Steve
    Cohen's Trade Secrets." *Bloomberg Markets Magazine*. Retrieved
    March 3, 2010 from
    http://www.bloomberg.com/news/2010.../steve-cohen-s-trade-
    secrets.html

13. Carnegie, Dale. (1991). *How to Develop Self-Confidence and
    Influence People*. New York, New York USA: Simon & Shuster, p.
    30.

14. Robert Greenleaf quotes. Retrieved March 16, 2010 from
    http://www.khabarexpress.com/Leadership_Robert-Greenleaf-
    quotes.html

15. Fromm, William. (1991). *Ten Commandments of Business and How
    to Break Them*. New York, New York USA: G.P. Putnam's Sons, p.
    13.

16. Emerson, Ralph Waldo quotes. Retrieved September 9, 2010 from
    http://www.iwise.com/3CUWV

17. Kanter, Rosabeth Moss. (2010). "Surprise! Four Strategies for
    Coping with Disruptions." Retrieved May 4, 2010 from
    http://blogs.hbr.org/kanter/2010/04/surprise-four-strategies-for-
    c.html

18. Selye, Hans. (1936). "The Nature of Stress" Retrieved April 4, 2010
    from http://www.icnr.com/articles/thenatureofstress.html

19. The American Institute of Stress. Retrieved April 4, 2010, from
    http://www.stress.html

20. Retrieved August 23, 2010 from
    http://www.bored.com/findquotes/cate_588.../Drinking.html

21. Wilcox, Ella Wheeler (1850–1919). "Solitude" Retrieved August 22, 2010 from http://www.poemhunter.com/poem/solitude/

22. Griffin, R. Morgan. "Give Your Body a Boost with Laughter" Retrieved May 25, 2010 from http://women.webmd.com/guide/give-your-body-boost-with-laughter

23. "Laughter is the Best Medicine." Retrieved August 10, 2010 from http://helpguide.org/

24. Retrieved August 27, 2010 from http://www.brainyquote.com/quotes/.../w/woodrowwil109722.html

25. Retrieved September 7, 2010 from http://www.ezinearticles.com

26. Drucker, Peter. (1954) *The Practice of Management*. Management by Objectives (MBO) and the SMART method first introduced.

27. *Smith, George David, & Dalzell, Frederick. (2000). Wisdom from the Robber Barons: Enduring Business Lessons from Rockefeller, Morgan, and the First Industrialists. New York, New York USA: Basic Books, p. 94.*

28. *Smith, George David, & Dalzell, Frederick. (2000). Wisdom from the Robber Barons: Enduring Business Lessons from Rockefeller, Morgan, and the First Industrialists. New York, New York USA: Basic Books, p. 95.*

29. Retrieved August 3, 2010 from http://www.1000ventures.com/business.../people_inspiring.html

30. Phillips, Bob. (1993). *Phillips' Book of Great Thoughts & Funny Sayings*. Wheaton, IL USA: Tyndale House Publishers, Inc., p. 90.

31. Retrieved August 17, 2010 from http://dictionary.reference.com/

32. Baldoni, John. (August 24, 2009). "Why Leaders Need Stories: A Lesson from Don Hewitt." Retrieved August 24, 2010 from http://www.blogs.hbr.org/baldoni/2009/

33. Fromm, William. (1991). *Ten Commandments of Business and How to Break* Them. New York, New York USA: G.P. Putnam's Sons, p. 42.

34. Big Dog's Learning Quotes. Retrieved June 27, 2010 from http://www.nwlink.com/~donclark/hrd/learnqt.html

35. Retrieved September 3, 2010 from www.famousquotesandauthors.com/.../role_models_quotes.html

Bibliography

Bennis, Warren, & Nanus, Burt. (1986). *Leaders*. New York, New York USA: Harper and Row.

Blanchard, Kenneth. (1981). *The One Minute Manager*. New York, New York USA: William Morrow and Company, Inc.

Burton, Katherine, & Effinger, Anthony. (Feb 26, 2010). "Steve Cohen's Trade Secrets." *Bloomberg Markets Magazine*.

Carnegie, Dale. (1991). *How to Develop Self-Confidence and Influence People*. New York, New York USA: Simon & Shuster.

Drucker, Peter F. (1954). *The Practice of Management*. London, England: William Heinemann Limited, Publishers.

Duncan, John C. (1911). *The Principles of Industrial Management*. New York, New York USA: D. Appleton and Company.

Fromm, William. (1991). *Ten Commandments of Business and How to Break Them*. New York, New York USA: G.P. Putnam's Sons.

Gawande, Atul. (2010). *The Checklist Manifesto: How to Get Things Right*. New York, New York USA: Metropolitan Books.

Gladwell, Malcolm. (2006). *Blink: The Power of Thinking Without Thinking*. New York, New York USA: Hachette Book Group.

Krass, Peter. (Ed.). (1997). *The Book of Business Wisdom*. Hoboken, NJ USA: John Wiley & Sons, Inc.

Machiavelli, Niccolò. (1513). *The Prince*. Florence, Italy.

Smith, Adam. (1976). The Wealth of Nations. Chicago, IL USA: The University of Chicago Press. (Originally published in 1776)

Smith, George David, & Dalzell, Frederick. (2000). Wisdom from the Robber Barons: Enduring Business Lessons from Rockefeller, Morgan, and the First Industrialists. New York. New York USA: Basic Books.

Sun Tza. (1991). *The Art of War*. Thomas Cleary (Trans.). Boston, MA USA: Shambhala Publications. (Original work published 6th century)

Tarbell, Ida. (1904). *The History of the Standard Oil Company*. New York, New York USA: *McClure's Magazine* (originally a series of articles).